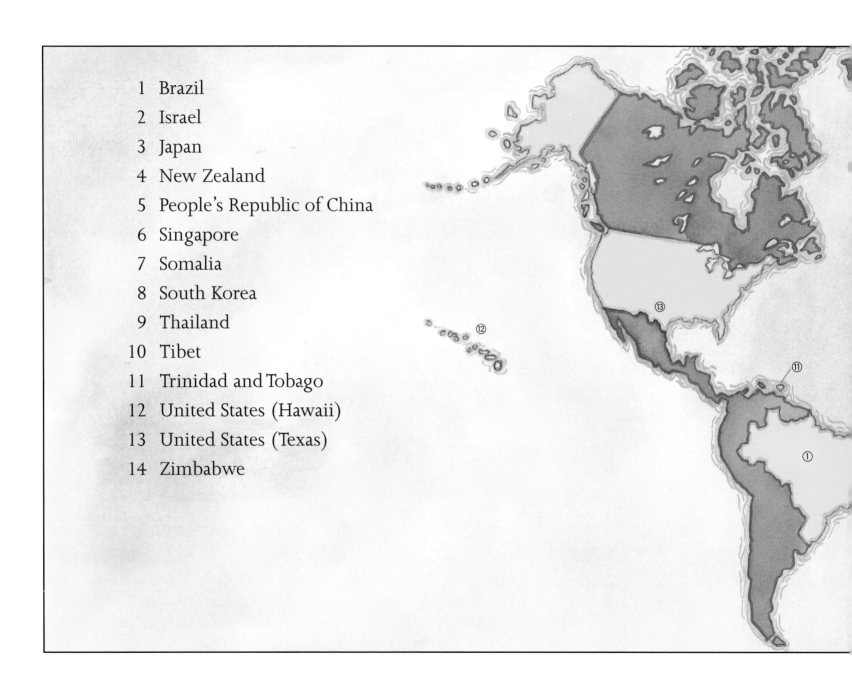

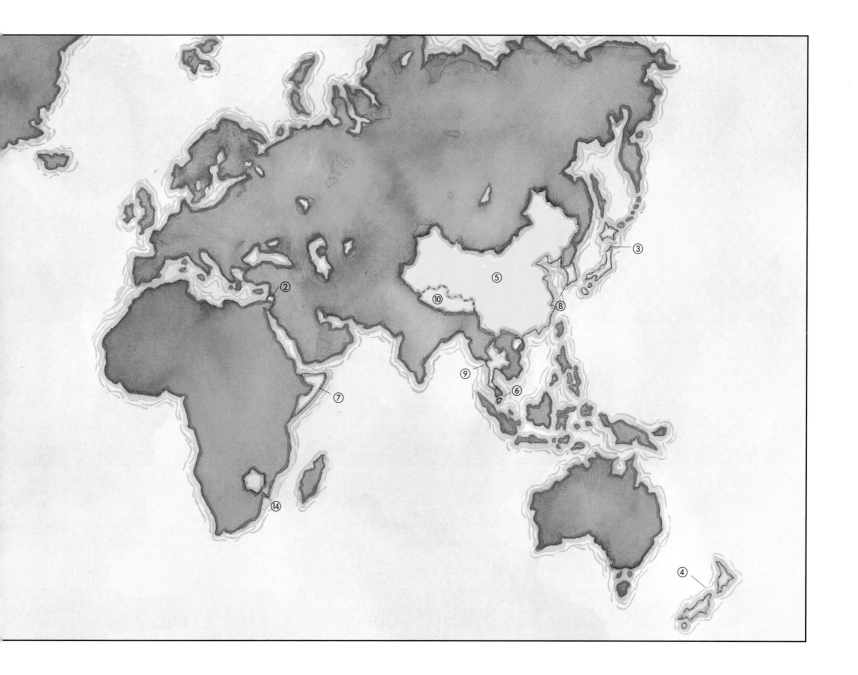

Dedicated to John Charles Briley, who will be my love forever and for two more days.

—M.D.L.

ACKNOWLEDGMENTS

All of you people, young and old, who were interested in this project, who gave me your ideas, your time, I thank you. I hope that with all of our efforts we can create a new generation of jacks players. I received assistance from the following people, who helped identify and describe different versions of jacks: Maria da Gloria Campello Soares Santana Seppy for Cinco Marias; Orna Raz and Shelly Sheaffer for Hamesh Avanim; Nancy Jo and George Spaulding, Ayumi Makita, Akiko Iwai, and Akane Okamoto for Otedama; Taowen Le for Zhua San; Toni Barila Thompson, Kimberley (C. J.) Thompson, T. J. Thompson, Chui-Fen "Kristy" Juzswik, and Jade Ruyi N. Juzswik for Five Stones; Mohamed Jilaow, Abdilahi Ibrahim, Yusuf Hussein, Faysall Ibrahim, Abdullah Abdulla, Waris Hersi, Gail Wilkinson, and Barbara Neal for Gariir; Carol Dunseth, Rob Rubis, Kuhn Siriluck, Hiri-O-Tappa, Kuhn Walaiporn Thamronglaohapan, Kuhn Saowanee Bunyaketu, and Kuhn Saengpetch Krutphan for Maakgep; Rinzing, Kathy, and Layne Lankford for Abhadhö; Diana Capriotti and Jean George for Trier; Nola Morgan, Kathy Cannallo, Mimi Wakeman, and Junko I. Nowaki for Kimo; Vanessa Bristow for Iguni; Cherie Clodfelter, the Oklahoma Jacks Champion; and John Briley, who helped with interviews and made life easier while I wrote.

The knucklebone recipe on page 38 was adapted from *Copycats & Artifacts*, by Marianne Ford. Reprinted by permission of David R. Godine, Publisher, Inc. Copyright © 1983 by Marianne Ford.

Watercolor, gouache, and colored pencils were used for the full-color illustrations. The text type is 13- and 14-point Joanna. Book design by Trish Parcell Watts.

Library of Congress Cataloging-in-Publication Data
Lankford, Mary D.
Jacks around the world/Mary D. Lankford; illustrated by Karen Dugan.
p. cm.
Includes bibliographical references and index.
Summary: Points out that this game, which is played with variations throughout the world, has been around for a long time and has a number of different names.
ISBN 0-688-13707-5 (trade)—ISBN 0-688-13708-3 (library)
1. Jacks (Game)—Juvenile literature.   [1. Jacks (Game).   2. Games.]
I. Dugan, Karen, ill.   II. Title.   GV1216.L35 1996   796.2—dc20
95-22864   CIP AC

Contents

Playing Jacks

What fun I have had, writing this book, playing detective, attempting to answer questions about a game I played as a child. Who invented jacks, where else is it played, how old is the game, and where did its name originate?

Researching these questions gave me a wonderful chance to learn about other people and their countries' traditions. In a taxi cab in Washington, D.C., I asked the driver where he lived as a young boy. He replied that he was from Somalia, which led to my discovery of Gariir, a game the driver had played many years ago in Africa. New immigrants, perhaps seeking relief from tragedies in their homeland of Somalia, found their way to Irving, Texas, and were responsive to my questions about the game. On an author visit to a school in Italy, I met three Japanese girls who demonstrated how they played Otedama. (Intriguingly, I could find no source for the origin of the game's first call-out of "*osala*," or "plate.") While on another speaking engagement I met an American woman and her family who had lived in Singapore. From a school report completed by the daughter I gained information on the country. I was then introduced to their Chinese friend, who had played Five Stones as a child.

Books, magazines, and artwork provided further information. From them, I learned that jacks, like most games, is not a new invention but a game with many variations on an ancient theme. Some people believe jacks was invented by Palamedes, a nobleman during the Trojan War who later taught the game to Greek soldiers. Others believe Asia, home of ancient civilizations, was the birthplace of jacks. A marble frieze dating from the first century A.D. was found in the ruins of Pompeii. This frieze shows women playing the game of jacks.

In ancient Rome, the game was called Tali. In China it was known as Jop Jee. The original name of the game, in the English language, may have been Chackstones, as it was called in England. This was probably taken from the English word for *pebble*, which is *chuck*. Today, most English-speaking children call the game Jacks, though it is also referred to as Jackstones, Dibs, Knucklebones, or Five Stones.

The rules may have changed slightly throughout history, or they may differ from country to country, but the game is basically the same. Pieces of bone, seeds, small rocks, or, today, pronged metal or plastic pieces represent the men, or jacks, of the game. In most games, an object, either a ball or stone, is tossed in the air. As the object is tossed, the pieces on the ground are picked up—first one at a time, then two at a time, and so on—before the airborne object falls to the ground or after one bounce of the ball. The game sounds very simple. However, the skill needed to toss, catch, and move objects requires practice. The challenge of becoming a champion is awaiting you.

Fundamentals of Play

Before you sample the games in this book, try onesies through sixies, the most basic version of jacks:

Throw six jacks onto the ground. *Using the same hand throughout,* toss the ball into the air, pick up one jack, then catch the ball before it bounces twice. Drop the jack to one side or transfer it to your other hand. Toss the ball again. Go on until you make a mistake or capture all six jacks. This is onesies.

In twosies, the jacks are picked up two at a time. Remember to use the same hand for tossing, picking up the jacks, and catching the ball. For threesies, pick up the jacks three at a time, and for foursies, pick up four jacks, then two. For fivesies, first five, then one. For sixies—pick up the six jacks all at once! If you make a mistake at any time, back you go to onesies.

In the directions for individual games, I've avoided boring repetition by assuming that you and your friends understand certain fundamentals for games in the jacks family. Unless the directions state otherwise, you must:

- use only one hand for basic movements
- keep your body in the same spot
- touch only the piece or pieces you are picking up
- pick up the correct number of pieces
- allow the ball to bounce only once
- catch a nonbouncing object before it hits the ground

Make a mistake on any of these and you lose your turn. When it is your turn again, you begin at the point in the game where you made your mistake.

The most common way to decide who goes first is to place the game pieces, the jacks, on the back of one hand. Toss the jacks into the air and catch them. Each player completes the toss, and the one who catches the greatest number goes first. If two players tie, they toss again. An easier variation is to use both hands and toss jacks from the palms to the backs of the hands. A more difficult variation is to toss from the palm of one hand to the back of the same hand, then back to the palm again. (Tips: Don't throw too high, and spread your fingers slightly to maximize the catching area.)

Another favorite way to determine who plays first is Stone, Scissors, Paper, which originated in Asia. In all variations of this game, two or three players raise their fists, moving them up and down as they count or chant the words for each of the three elements of the game. The third time the fist is raised, all players make a sign with their hand for either stone (fist), scissors (index and third finger pointed together, others folded back toward the palm), or paper (hand flat, fingers together, palm down). Stone can break scissors. Scissors can cut paper. Paper can cover stone. The person with the strongest sign plays first. If all players make the same sign, the game is played again.

In the United States, players chant "one, two, three." It might be fun to try the Chinese chant "ching, chang, pok" or the Japanese words "ishi, hasami, kami," which mean "stone, scissors, paper."

The best way to get better at any jacks game is to practice. These are a few techniques that will help you improve your game. Try to space the jacks when you toss them. If you are picking up by ones, you will want the jacks farther apart; if you're picking up eleven pieces, you'll want the jacks close together. Make sure you position yourself comfortably so you aren't too far away from the pieces or too close. Find a tossing style that makes the ball or stone go straight up and down, so you will always know where your hand should be for catching. The idea is to get the ball or stone high enough to give you time to pick up the jacks but not so high that you lose control of it. Good luck!

 **Brazil**

Cinco Marias

Brazil, slightly smaller than the United States, shares boundaries with all but two of the twelve other South American countries. Crossed in the north by the equator and in the south by the tropic of Capricorn, this mammoth country has a coastline of 4,603 miles and is home to a significant length of the world's second-longest river, the 4,000-mile-long Amazon.

In the crowded city streets, children collect flat smooth stones from parks or roadsides to use as game pieces. Stones are chosen not necessarily for size, but because they feel good in the hand. Sometimes favorite stones are kept in a small bag or have the owner's initials carved on them. The simple game of Cinco Marias (Five Marys) is popular with boys and girls as young as four or five. Two, three, or four play together.

How to Play:

1. Toss five stones to the ground and select one.

2. Toss the selected stone into the air, pick up one stone from the ground, then catch the airborne stone. Continue until you have picked up all the stones.

3. Follow the same pattern for rounds two, three, and four, scooping up by twos, threes, and then fours. Continue play until your turn is lost.

4. The first player to pick up all four stones is the winner.

Variation: *A Visita Mamãe Casa de Mamãe (A Visit to Mom's House)*

2. Hold your nontossing hand palm downward, slightly above the ground. Place your thumb and index finger on the ground in a **V** shape.

3. Toss the stone, and push one of the stones on the ground into the opening of the **V** shape. (You may decide to allow two tries for this move.) Continue play as before, pushing by ones, then twos, and so on, until all the stones have been pushed between your two fingers.

4. Take turns and score as in Cinco Marias.

 **Israel**

Hamesh Avanim

Although the State of Israel was created in 1948, its streets and buildings are constant reminders of the land's rich historical past. Israel's flag, too, with the Star of David and stripes, symbolic of a Hebrew prayer shawl, reflects the country's dedication to remembering its religious heritage.

Israeli children attend school from Sunday through Friday. Saturday is the Hebrew day of rest, a chance for *yeled* (boys) and *yalda* (girls) to play Hamesh Avanim (Five Stones). The game is played with five gold-colored cubes, or if these are not available, the game can be played with stones or pebbles. A challenging pastime for one or several players, Hamesh Avanim has various versions throughout the region. Here is one variation.

How to Play:

1. Gently throw all five stones on the ground. Select one and place it on your palm. While you toss this stone from your palm to the back of the same hand, pick up as many of the stones on the ground as possible. Since this is difficult, most players attempt to pick up only one stone at a time. Continue until no stones remain on the ground.

2. Play round two the same way with one exception: You must now flip and catch two stones while picking up as many as possible from the ground.

3. In round three, repeat the pattern, this time tossing and catching three stones.

4. For the last round, place four stones in your palm. Toss these and try to catch them as you pick up the remaining stone.

5. The player who successfully completes all four rounds wins.

 **Japan**

Otedama

Japan is sometimes called "the land of the rising sun," since to Asian peoples looking eastward the sun does appear to rise over the islands of Japan. In Japanese, the country and its people are frequently referred to as *Nippon* or *Nihon*, meaning "source of the sun."

Many elements of Japanese life are based on simplicity, including art and poetry. The simple Japanese game, originating in the ninth century, that most resembles the western version of jacks is Otedama (from *te*, meaning "hand," and *dama*, meaning "ball"). Otedama is usually played by two, three, or four girls, with almost any number of small silk bags loosely filled with rice or beads. For our game, use nine bags, including a chief, or parent, bag, which is the same size as the others but usually made of a different fabric pattern.

How to Play:

1. Toss the bags into the air. Catch the chief bag, and let all others fall to the floor. Call out "*osala*," or "plate," as you do so.

2. For round one, say "*ohitotsu*," or "one," as you toss the chief bag into the air, pick up one of the bags from the floor, and catch the chief bag again. Repeat until all bags have been picked up. Say "*ohitotsu*" each time, except for when you pick up the final bag, when you call out "*osala*" again.

3. In round two, pick up two bags following each toss of the chief bag. Say "*ofutatsu*," or "two," as you pick up the first three pairs. Repeat "*osala*" as the last two bags are picked up.

4. Continue the pattern in round three. Say "*omittsu*," or "three," as the two trios of bags are picked up. With the last two bags, say "*ofutatsu okoshite osala*," or "two remaining."

5. In the final round, pick up four bags each time. Repeat "*oyottsu*," or "four," with each pick-up. After the second catch, hold up the chief bag by itself and say "*nokoshite*," or "one remaining."

6. The player who first completes the four rounds is the winner.

Huripapa

When the first humans, the Maori, arrived in New Zealand, they found a land of birds, trees, and magnificent vegetation but no animal life. The land was called *Aotearo* by the Maori, which means "land of the long white cloud." Now a minority population, the Maori continue to maintain many customs and traditions, including decorating their buildings with beautiful wood carvings.

Another such tradition is the game of Huripapa. Its origins are unclear. It may have been played long before European settlers came to New Zealand, or possibly it was introduced to the Maori by European whalers. Whatever its origins, this jacks-type game was played with peach stones or the knucklebones of sheep. In this region, sheep have always been abundant, and their bones easily found in the countryside. After finding these bones, Maori children scrubbed and polished them and sometimes used onion skins to dye them brown. Boys and girls of European and Maori descent still play many jacks-type games. The following variations of Huripapa use five knucklebones or stones.

How to Play:

Variation: *Jump the Ladder*

1. Place four bones on the ground, lined up like steps in a ladder.

2. Toss the remaining bone in the air, and use your index finger to jump over the nearest bone. Catch the bone with the same hand. Continue to jump single bones until you reach the top of the ladder. Repeat, jumping two bones at a time.

3. The first player to jump all four bones wins.

Variation: *Polly Put the Kettle On*

1. Throw all bones to the ground. Select one bone to toss.

2. With each toss, move three of the other bones, one by one, to form a triangle shape.

3. The first player to place the fourth bone—the kettle—on top, centered on the other three bones, is the winner.

Zhua San

China's border touches more than a dozen other countries and encloses a land of deserts, mountains, and grassland plains. This vast land is home to over one billion people, the largest population of any country in the world.

Many important inventions were Chinese, including paper, the suspension bridge, gunpowder, the seismograph, the compass, and, perhaps, the game of jacks. Today, in eastern central China, boys and girls play Zhua San (Pickup Three). Any number can play, but usually there are two to four players, each with nine small stones.

How to Play:

1. To determine who goes first, pool all players' stones together. Take turns tossing these stones from the palm of one hand to the back of the same hand and again to the palm. Whoever catches the most stones begins play, the person with the next largest catch is second, and so on. If there's a tie for the winner, those players must toss again.

2. Hold all stones from all players in one hand and toss them into the air. You must catch at least two stones on the back of the same hand. Otherwise you are "starved to death" and lose your turn.

3. Toss the stones caught on the back of your hand into the air, and catch exactly one in your palm or with your fingers, palm facing upward. If you don't catch any stones, your turn ends. If you catch more than two stones, you are "fed up to death" and lose your turn. If you catch exactly two stones, the other players place the extra stone on the ground, usually somewhere that will make sweeping up, the next step, more difficult.

4. Now toss the single stone into the air, sweep up three stones from the ground in one smooth motion, and catch the falling stone.

5. One of the four stones in your hand is considered won and is set aside. Toss the remaining three into the air, repeating steps 2 through 4. If you lose your turn, begin your next turn at step 2.

6. Eventually all but three stones, two on the ground and one in a player's hand, will have been won. At that point, sweep up the remaining two, setting one aside as before.

7. Now only two stones are left. Toss one and sweep up the last. Finally, toss this last stone into the air, catching it on the back of your hand and then in your palm.

8. After all stones have been won, the player with the most stones wins the game.

 # Singapore

Five Stones

Singapore, Asia's smallest independent state, consists of one large island, twenty-six miles long and fourteen miles wide, and over fifty smaller islands. Its population is so diverse that there are four official languages: Mandarin Chinese, Malay, Tamil, and English. Because Singapore is only eighty-seven miles north of the equator, it has a year-round summer climate. For Singapore's children a cool cement surface, porch, or school cafeteria can provide a place for groups of two to six to sit and play Five Stones. The game is played in the center of a circle, using one set of five handmade triangular-shaped cloth bags (called stones) that are loosely filled with rice, sand, or saga seeds (small, hard red seeds from tropical trees). Since some steps in this game are almost like juggling, it takes practice, skill, and good hand-eye coordination to play.

How to Play:

1. Toss all five stones on the ground. Pick up one stone, toss it up, pick up another stone, and catch the airborne stone. Continue until all four have been picked up.

2. Repeat step 1, picking up two stones at a time.

3. Repeat step 1, picking up first three stones, then one.

4. Repeat step 1, picking up all four stones in one sweep.

5. With all stones in one hand, toss one into the air, place the remaining four on the ground, and catch the airborne stone. Then toss the same stone, pick up the four on the ground, and catch the airborne stone.

6. Toss all the stones on the ground, and pick up any two. Toss one of these two stones into the air while you exchange the stone remaining in your hand for any other stone on the ground. Repeat until all three stones on the ground have been exchanged.

7. Toss the two stones in your hand into the air. Catch one of these in the nonthrowing hand. At the same time, pick up any stone from the ground with the tossing hand, then catch the airborne stone. Continue until you have picked up all the stones on the ground, and you have three stones in one hand and two stones in the other. Again, toss the two stones in your throwing hand, catching one stone in each hand.

Finally, toss the single stone in your throwing hand, transfer the four other stones to this hand, and catch the airborne stone.

8. Toss all five stones on the ground. Let an opponent select the stone to be tossed. Arrange the remaining stones so that two are touching and are in between the other two. The stones should look like this: O OO O. Then toss the selected stone into the air, pick up the two touching stones, and catch the airborne stone.

Now choose one of the played stones to be the tosser, and set the others aside. Toss the selected stone in the air, sweep up the two remaining stones, and catch the airborne stone.

9. Toss all five stones on the ground. Let an opponent select the stone to be tossed. Toss the chosen stone, sweep up all the remaining stones, and catch the falling stone.

10. Repeat step 8, except this time pick up the two outer stones.

11. Score one point for every successfully completed step. At the game's end, the highest scorer wins.

Somalia

Gariir

The coastline of this tropical East African country, more than 1,700 miles long, extends into the Indian Ocean and forms a point called the Horn of Africa. Civil wars and strife have marred the country's recent history, but the rich heritage of this region is centuries old. From here may have come the gifts of frankincense and myrrh described in many accounts of the birth of Christ.

Gariir is the name of a jacks game played by Somali boys and girls, and it is also the signal for who will play first. By calling out the word "*gariir*" as you approach a potential player, you gain the first turn. Alternatively, a question is sometimes asked: "*Gacan, Ilaney, yaa ka weyn?*" This translates as "Who has a bigger hand than the hand of God?"

The game may include two or more players. In turn, each player places twelve pebbles in a small *god*, or shallow hole in the ground. The *god* should be just large enough to contain the twelve pebbles. In contrast to the rules for many other games of jacks, those for Gariir allow you to touch or move pebbles in the *god* as you try to remove the correct number. Your turn ends when you fail to catch the "leader" pebble, and you must begin again at the count at which you dropped the leader.

How to Play:

1. Select one pebble to be the leader. This stone should be rounder and a little heavier than the twelve pebbles in the *god*.

2. Toss the leader into the air, remove one pebble from the *god*, and catch the leader. If you remove too many pebbles, you can toss the leader again and return the extra pebbles to the *god*.

3. Continue until you have removed all the pebbles one by one.

4. Repeat for the second round, this time removing the pebbles two by two.

5. Repeat for round three, removing three each time. The player who successfully removes all the pebbles, three at a time, from the *god* is the winner.

Kong-Keui

In 1945 the country of Korea, formerly a single kingdom, was divided into what are now known as the countries of North Korea (the Democratic People's Republic of Korea) and South Korea (the Republic of Korea). These two countries share a peninsula on the coast of China bordered by the Sea of Japan on the east and the Yellow Sea on the west. To the east of Korea are the islands of Japan and to the north and west is China.

During the dry winter months, boys use five small stones to play a three-round game called Kong-Keui. The increasingly difficult rounds are called *al-nat-ki*, *al-hpoum-ki*, and *al-kka-ki*, which mean "laying the eggs," "setting the eggs," and "hatching the eggs."

How to Play:

1. Toss four stones on the ground. Toss the fifth stone into the air, pick up one stone from the ground, and catch the tossed stone.

2. Set aside the picked-up stone, and repeat until all the "eggs" have been "laid."

3. For round two, place one hand, palm downward, on the ground next to four stones.

4. Toss the remaining stone with the other hand. Before you catch the tossed stone, push one of the stones on the ground under your palm.

5. Continue tossing and moving stones until all the "eggs" have been "set."

6. For round three, place three stones on the ground. Set one aside to toss. Curl the little finger of your tossing hand and place the remaining stone in the crook of the finger.

7. Toss the stone, tap one of the stones on the ground with the stone held in your little finger, and catch the tossed stone.

8. Repeat until all three stones have been tapped, or "hatched."

9. The first person to complete all three rounds is the winner.

Thailand

Maakgep

Unlike many of its neighboring Asian countries, Thailand has never been a European colony. In 1939 the name of the country was changed from Siam to Thailand, which means "land of the free." Thailand is a mix of jungles, rain forests, mountains, and so many fields of rice that the country exports over four thousand tons of rice each year. Its capital city, Bangkok, is home to five million people.

During the rainiest season, between May and October, Thai girls stay indoors and play a game called Maakgep. The game is played with five stones per player. The stones are chosen to match the size of a player's hands. Before play begins, the total point count for the game, sometimes twenty, is determined.

How to Play:

1. Throw all five stones to the ground and select one.

2. On every toss of the selected stone, pick up a single stone from the ground. After the toss, set the played stone aside.

3. Continue play until all four stones have been picked up and set aside. Scoop up all five stones in your palm, toss them into the air, and try to catch as many as possible on the back of the same hand. The number you catch determines the number of points earned on that round.

4. On the second round, repeat steps 1 through 3, picking up two stones at a time.

5. Continue play until the winning score is reached, first picking up a set of three stones, then one, then all four. If this becomes too easy, play the game in the same manner but retain the picked-up stones in the palm of your tossing hand instead of setting them aside. If no player has reached the winning score, go back to the first round of play.

Variation (*for younger children*)

2. Place the selected stone on the back of your tossing hand. Holding the stone steady, use your thumb and index finger to pick up one stone from the ground.

3. Lightly toss the balanced stone from the back of your hand to your palm, retaining the stone that has been picked up from the ground. Set that stone aside, and repeat until all four stones have been picked up.

4. Continue play by picking up two stones at a time, then three, and finally four.

 **Tibet**

Abhadhö

Because it is the world's largest and highest plateau, Tibet is sometimes known as "the roof of the world." For centuries, as China fought to control Tibet, its peaceful people have struggled to maintain their independence. Even now, as part of the People's Republic of China, Tibet maintains with determination its ancient customs and devotion to Buddhism.

Today nomads continue to live in the mountains and tend herds of sheep and goats. To break the monotony, the boys and girls who care for the animals play Abhadhö, which translates as *abha*, or "many ways of grabbing," and *dho*, or "stones." The game (with variations) is usually played by one to five players using five stones, peach seeds, or the knee bones of goats. In the Tibetan culture it is particularly the case that determining the winner is not as important as enjoying the game.

How to Play:

1. Toss all five stones on the ground.

2. Take one stone from the ground, toss it into the air, pick up a single stone from the ground, and catch the falling stone. As you toss the stone, say the words "*yha dho*," or "going up." As it descends say "*madho*," or "going down."

3. Continue play until you have picked up all the stones one by one and then two by two.

4. Round three repeats as in step 2, except that an opponent decides which three stones you must pick up. Then pick up the remaining stone.

5. Round four repeats as in step 2, except that you pick up all four stones at once.

6. To end the game, toss all five stones into the air and catch them on the back of your hand.

Variation: *Samba (Bridge)*

2. With your nonthrowing hand, touch the ground lightly with your fingertips, palm raised, forming a bridge.

3. With each toss of the stone, push another stone under the bridge until all four have been moved.

4. To end the game, toss all the stones in the air and catch them on the back of your hand. If any fall to the ground, balance the remaining stones on the back of your hand while picking up those from the ground with your thumb and index finger. Repeat the toss until you have caught all the stones on the back of your hand.

Variation: *Szima (Hooks)*

2. With your nonthrowing hand, make the bridge position, spreading your fingers apart to resemble the talons of a bird.

3. With each toss of the stone, push a stone between a gap in your fingers, using a different gap for each toss. The stones may touch one another underneath your palm.

4. When you have collected all four stones, remove your talon hand. With your playing hand, toss the stone and pick up the rest from the ground before catching the tossed stone.

5. Finally, toss all five stones on the ground again. This time an opponent selects which stone you pick up first.

6. Continue play until you have picked up all the stones by ones, twos, and threes.

Trinidad and Tobago

Trier

Centuries ago, the islands of Trinidad and Tobago drifted away from the coast of South America to become part of the chain of Caribbean islands known as the Lesser Antilles. The islands' first inhabitants, the Amerindians, called Trinidad *Lere*, meaning "island," or, possibly, "land of the hummingbird," for its numerous species of birds, including the rare white-tailed Sabrewing hummingbird. When Columbus, in 1498, first saw the islands, he named Trinidad for its trinity of three prominent mountain peaks.

Because people of many cultures live on Trinidad and its twin, Tobago, these islands are sometimes called the Rainbow Country. This cultural diversity may explain the rules for playing the island game of Trier, whose origins may be traced to a game played in Africa, India, Europe, China, and other countries. It is a three-round game for two or more players that uses five beans or small stones.

How to Play:

1. Toss all five beans (or stones) from the palm of one hand to the back of the same hand.
2. Toss the beans caught on the back of your hand and catch them in the palm of the same hand. If any beans are dropped on this toss, no points are scored. If all the beans are successfully tossed and caught, one point is scored for each.
3. Continue play for two more rounds, repeating steps 1 and 2.
4. At the end of three rounds, the player with the highest score wins.

United States (Hawaii)

Kimo

The mountainous islands of the northern Pacific Ocean make up America's fiftieth state. The Hawaiian state flag has eight stripes, symbolizing the eight islands, the largest of which is called Hawaii. Millions of tourists travel to Hawaii each year to enjoy the beauty of the mountains and to swim in or ride the waves of the surf. From the beaches, boys and girls of all ages collect 'ili'ili, rocks that have been worn down by ocean or river waters into small rounded pebbles. These objects are used to play the centuries-old game of Kimo, or Jackstones.

Early Hawaiian chiefs often played Kimo on a headland (a piece of land that extends out into the water), called *lae-kimo*. The word *kimo* means "to bob" and describes the movement of spectators' and players' heads as they play the game. Kimo is usually played by two people sitting on a woven mat with a pile of about one hundred 'ili'ili between them. These stones are now referred to as the *'ai*. Each player may bring his own special *kimo*, the pebble to be tossed, or may choose a pebble, slightly larger than the others, from the *'ai*. In this game, your turn does not end if you move pebbles in the pile during play.

How to Play:

1. Toss the *kimo* into the air, pick up one pebble from the pile of *'ai*, and catch the *kimo* before it falls to the ground. Place to the side the pebble you just picked up, or earned.

2. Continue to pick up one pebble at a time. Failure to pick up a pebble or to catch the *kimo* ends your turn.

3. After both players have played and all the pebbles of the *'ai* have been won, the player with the most *'ai* wins the game.

 # United States (Texas)

Jacks

Throughout the history of Texas, long considered valuable territory, six different flags have flown over its farmlands, forests, mountains, and arid expanses. The Texas I knew as a child was the largest of our forty-eight states. The 1959 addition of Hawaii and Alaska to the Union not only changed the number of states but ended my boast of living in the largest one.

In my youth, the hot northern Texas summers were spent without air-conditioning. To escape the heat we looked for a cool place to sit and play games like Pickup Sticks, Chinese Checkers, and Jacks. The rules we used for Jacks in its many variations have been followed by generations of American boys and girls. You will probably recognize them.

For the basic game you need a small ball, six jacks, and a flat surface for bouncing the ball. Any number can play, but you can also play alone just to improve your skills.

How to Play:

Variation: *Pigs in the Pen*

1. Toss all the jacks on the ground.

2. Curve your nonthrowing hand, fingers together, into a cup shape, or "pigpen." Rest the side of your palm and of your little finger on the ground. After tossing the ball, slide the jacks, one by one, into the pen instead of picking them up.

3. Repeat this pattern by twos, threes, and so on up to sixes. The first player to complete the game wins.

Variation: *Sheep over the Fence*

2. Rest the side of your nonthrowing hand, fingers together and straight, on the ground. This is your "fence." When you toss the ball, jump the jacks, or "sheep," from one side of the fence to the other. Repeat this pattern, as before.

Variation: *Bees in the Hive*

2. Make a "beehive" with your nonthrowing hand, holding it palm down with fingers and thumb spread apart and fingertips touching the ground.

3. Toss the ball and move the jacks, one at a time, into any of the spaces between your fingers.

4. Lift your beehive without moving the jacks. Toss the ball and, with your tossing hand, pick up all six jacks.

5. Throw the jacks on the ground, and put your beehive in place again.

6. Continue moving jacks—two through five at a time—repeating step 4 after each round. For twosies through fivesies choose a different space between your fingers each time jacks are pushed into your beehive.

7. The first person to finish sixies is the winner.

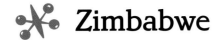

Zimbabwe

Iguni

Formerly known as Rhodesia, and once a colony of Great Britain, this African country was renamed Zimbabwe when it achieved independence in 1980. Zimbabwe's northern boundary is marked by the Zambezi River, which flows into the towering Victoria Falls. The Limpopo River, along the southern border, is the site, according to legend, where the elephant child got its trunk.

In Zimbabwe, girls between the ages of five and eighteen play a game called Iguni by the Ndebele tribe and Katé by the Venda tribe. The game pieces are twelve small pebbles, easily held in the hand and, preferably, roundish. One of the pebbles is used for tossing and the rest are placed evenly around the edge of a shallow hole in the ground, about two to three inches wide. Iguni is played most often by children living in the country, but it is also a pastime of schoolchildren in the city.

How to Play:

1. The game is played in rounds. In the first round, throw the tossing pebble into the air, knock one pebble into the hole, and catch the airborne pebble again. Continue play until all eleven pebbles are in the hole.

2. Complete the round by tossing the twelfth pebble and removing all eleven pebbles from the hole in one move. If you are unsuccessful at any stage, you lose your turn, and you must start again from round one.

3. The second round is the same as the first, except you knock two pebbles at a time into the hole. A single pebble will be left over at the end. Following the pebble toss, pick up and place the leftover pebble in the hole instead of knocking it in.

4. The third round continues the pattern, with two pebbles left over at the end. Place them in the hole just as in round two.

5. Continue play until round eleven, when all pebbles are knocked into the hole in one toss. The first player to complete this round wins.

6. You can play a championship round in which the first three players to complete eleven rounds compete against one another.

How to Make Knucklebones

Children from New Zealand and sometimes China have traditionally played jacks with the knucklebones of sheep. These roundish knobby bones make excellent playing pieces. You can make your own knucklebones by following this simple recipe. Having an adult nearby is the best safety precaution.

You will need:

12 tablespoons plain flour
2 tablespoons salt
1 teaspoon glycerin (available at most drugstores)
3 tablespoons cold water (plus 1 teaspoon, if needed)
Measuring spoons (tablespoon and teaspoon)
2 mixing bowls
Hard flat surface that can be cleaned
Popsicle stick
Pencil with point broken off
Wire rack

1. Mix the flour and salt together in a mixing bowl. In the other bowl, add the glycerin to the water.

2. Stir the glycerin/water mixture gradually into the dry ingredients until the dough comes cleanly away from the sides of the bowl. If it does not hold together, add 1 teaspoon water.

3. Take a heaping teaspoon of the dough and roll it in the palms of your hands, making it round and compact.

4. Put the dough on a flat surface and press it down with your finger until it is about half an inch thick.

5. Holding the flattened sides with your thumb and forefinger, make two grooves in the dough about three-fourths of the way around with a Popsicle stick.

6. Flatten the untouched part into a base, so the knucklebone is freestanding.

7. If you wish, using a pencil with the point broken off, you can make four indentations on the base, as shown, and on the sides of your knucklebone.

8. Put the pieces carefully on the wire rack. Leave them to harden for two to three days in a warm dry place.